INSIDE BATTLE MACHINES

FIGHTER PLANES

Thanks to the creative team:

Senior Editor: Alice Peebles
Picture Research: Nic Dean
Fact Checking: Tom Jackson
Illustration: Mat Edwards and Victor Mclindon
Design: www.collaborate.agency

First published in Great Britain in 2017
by Hungry Tomato Ltd
PO Box 181
Edenbridge
Kent, TN8 9DP

A CIP catalogue record for this book is available
from the British Library.

ISBN 978-1-910684-25-2

Printed and bound in China

Discover more at
www.hungrytomato.com

INSIDE BATTLE MACHINES
FIGHTER PLANES

The "Flying Bedstead", used for experimenting with vertical take-off in the 1950s

by Chris Oxlade

HUNGRY TOMATO.

The Supermarine Spitfire was one of the best fighter planes of World War II.

Contents

Fighter Planes   6

First Fighters   8

World War 1 Advances   10

Battle of Britain Fighters   12

P-51 Mustang   14

First Jet Fighters   16

Stealthy Machines   18

At the Controls   20

Targeting Weapons   22

Attack Helicopters   24

F-35 Fighter   26

Timeline and Fact File   28

Glossary   30

Index   32

[Highlighted words appear in the glossary]

BATTLE MACHINES
FIGHTER PLANES

Modern fighter planes are super-fast, super-loud and super-complex battle machines, crammed with clever technology. Fighter planes battle each other to control the air, because **air superiority** gives one side in a conflict a big advantage. Most modern fighters also have other roles, such as attacking enemy forces on the ground.

Fighter types

Today the term 'fighter' can mean several different sorts of planes, which carry out different missions. Many planes can be adapted to do different jobs.

Air superiority fighter A fighter designed to engage enemy aircraft and gain control of the air

Strike fighter A fighter that also attacks ground targets

Multirole combat aircraft A fighter that performs various roles, including air-to-air combat

Old versus new

Two types of aircraft here show how the technology of fighters has changed over the last 100 years! Above right is a Sopwith Triplane from World War I (1914–18), the first war to feature fighter planes. Below left and right is a Lockheed Martin F-22 Raptor, a super-modern fighter. Its structure, engine, controls and weapons would be unrecognizable to a Sopwith Triplane pilot.

F-22 Raptor

The Lockheed Martin F-22 Raptor is a state-of-the-art air superiority fighter. It is fast, agile and stealthy, with air-to-air and air-to-ground weapons.

Sopwith Triplane

The Sopwith was a single-seater with three sets of wings. It was a favourite among pilots for its agility.

FIRST
FIGHTERS

The first successful powered planes flew in the early years of the 20th century. World War I began just a decade later, in 1914. Armies on both sides realized that planes would help them see enemy positions. So the first military planes were actually scout planes. It wasn't long before these planes were armed with machine guns, and went on missions to hunt down enemy scouts. The fighter plane was born.

Airco DH.2

Length: 7.7 metres

Wingspan: 8.6 metres

Weight: 428 kilograms

Engine: Gnome rotary

Top speed: 150 kilometres per hour

Ceiling: 4,265 metres

Armament: 1 x Lewis gun

Number built: 453

First flight: July 1915

Pusher planes

Many of the first fighters had a propeller at the back, behind the cockpit, as in this Airco DH.2. The planes were called 'pushers' because the propeller pushed them along. This layout allowed the pilot to sit in the front of the fuselage and fire his gun forwards without hitting the propeller.

Rotary power

The **rotary engine** was the most popular engine for fighter planes in World War I. A rotary engine was a type of piston engine, in which pistons moved up and down in cylinders. In most engines, the cylinders stay still, and the pistons turn a crankshaft. A rotary engine is built in reverse. The crankshaft stays still and the cylinders and pistons spin round with the propeller.

Cylinders spin round, making the propeller spin

Crankshaft

Piston

The Wright Flyer

Orville and Wilbur Wright's Flyer was the first plane to make a controlled, powered flight, in the United States in 1903. Before this, flights had been in gliders (with no engines), or just short, uncontrolled hops.

Balloon attacks

Before and during World War I, armies sent observers up in gas-filled observation balloons to spy on enemy positions. These balloons were an easy target for the fighter planes, which could shoot holes in the balloons. The balloons often caught fire as they sank to the ground.

WORLD WAR 1
ADVANCES

As World War I continued, both sides designed and built better and better fighter planes. The technology of planes improved quickly. Engines became lighter in weight, but more powerful. Aircraft frames became lighter, but stronger. So planes became faster and more manoeuvrable. Most fighters had only one seat, so the pilot both flew the plane and fired the guns.

Fokker Dr.1

Most planes were **biplanes**. They had two sets of wings, one above the other, linked by **struts** (vertical rods) and wires. This made a strong box-like structure. There were also **triplanes**, with three sets of wings. The most famous type of triplane was the Fokker Dr.1, flown by the famous German fighter pilot Manfred von Richthofen (known as the Red Baron). It could turn tightly and climb steeply, and was one of the best fighters of World War I.

Firing through the propeller

The first single-seat planes had guns mounted on the wing above the cockpit, so that bullets missed the spinning propeller. But the best place for a gun to be placed in a single-seat fighter was in front of the cockpit, where the pilot could look along it to aim, and where he could reach it in case it jammed. So engineers invented interrupter gear or synchro gear, which stopped the gun from firing if a propeller blade was in the path of a bullet.

The Chandelle: turning 180° while climbing steeply

The spin: diving and rolling to lose altitude quickly

The half roll: rolling then diving to turn back

Dogfight tricks

Combat pilots fought each other in dogfights, making their planes dive, roll and turn to try to get into position to attack, or to escape from an attacker. Pilots invented attacking and defensive manoeuvres.

Eddie Rickenbacker

Life as a World War I pilot was dangerous. Many pilots were shot down after only a few flights. But some were very successful, and shot down dozens of enemy planes. Among these fighter **aces** was US pilot Eddie Rickenbacker. He shot down 26 planes, and lived to tell the tale.

The Battle of Britain was a fight for command of the skies over Britain in the summer of 1940, during World War II (1939–45). The Luftwaffe (the German air force) sent bombers to attack British ships, airfields and factories. British fighters tried to stop the bombers from reaching their targets, and German fighters tried to protect the bombers.

SUPERMARINE SPITFIRE

Length: 9.1 metres

Wingspan: 11.2 metres

Weight: 2.3 tonnes

Engine: Rolls-Royce Merlin or Griffin

Top speed: 595 kilometres per hour

Ceiling: 11,125 metres

Armament: Hispano cannon / Browning machine gun

Number built: 20,351

First flight: March 1936

Supermarine Spitfire

By the time World War II began, most fighters were made of metal; were **monoplanes**, with just one set of wings; and had **in-line engines** or **radial engines** instead of rotary engines. The Supermarine Spitfire could climb high, powered by its Rolls-Royce Merlin or Griffin engine. It was armed with cannon in the wings that fired explosive shells.

Cockpit controls

A glass canopy protected a Spitfire's cockpit from the wind and cold. There were controls to steer the plane through the air and to work the engine and other parts. Instruments showed the plane's speed, **altitude**, fuel level and so on.

Throttle controlled engine power

Altimeter showed height above ground

Air speed indicator

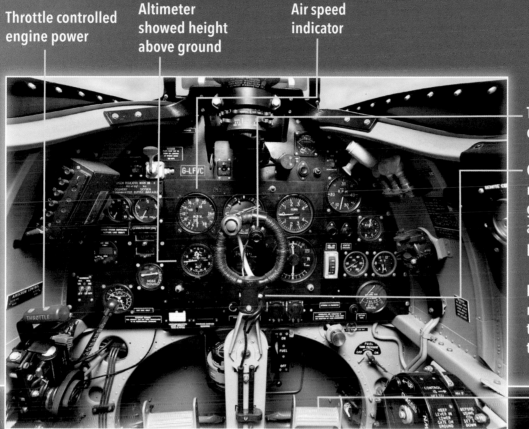

Trigger for cannon

Control stick made the nose go up or down, and made the plane roll

Rudder pedals made the plane turn from side to side

Messerschmitt Bf 109

The BF 109 was Germany's best World War II fighter, closely matching the Allies' Spitfire. It had an all-metal body and foldaway undercarriage. Nearly 34,000 were built. The aircraft played a big role in Germany's early victories, and could be both an out-and-out fighter and a ground-attack machine.

P-51 MUSTANG

The Mustang joined World War II late, but it played an important role in the victory for Britain, the USA and their allies. This American single-seat fighter was one of the War's most advanced aircraft. In Europe it defended American bombers against German fighters on long-**range** raids over Germany, and attacked German airfields. In the Pacific it took on Japan's superb fighter, the Mitsubishi A6M Zero.

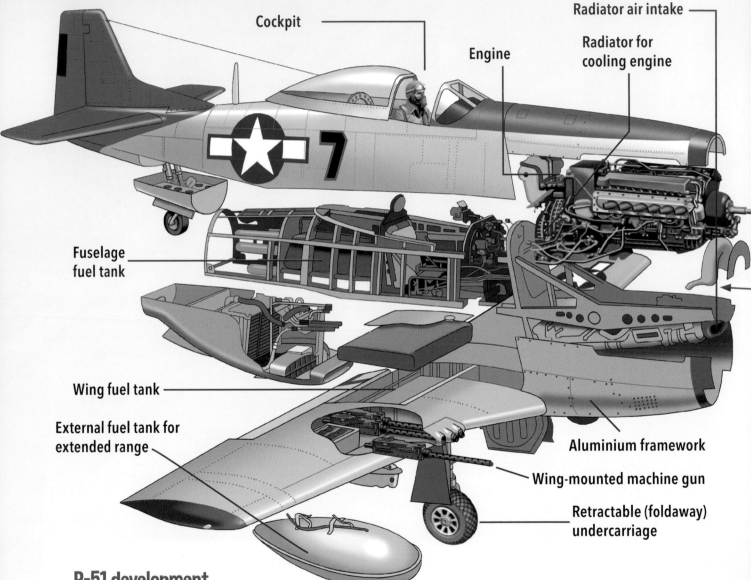

Cockpit

Engine

Radiator air intake

Radiator for cooling engine

Fuselage fuel tank

Wing fuel tank

External fuel tank for extended range

Aluminium framework

Wing-mounted machine gun

Retractable (foldaway) undercarriage

P-51 development

The P-51 Mustang was built by North American Aviation. It was first developed for Britain's RAF, which needed fighters early in the war. The prototype first flew in October 1940. Its main features were a thin, efficient wing, a smooth **fuselage** with low **drag**, and an all-aluminium frame and skin. It could also carry fuel tanks on its wings to improve its range. The first Mustang entered service with the RAF in January 1942. It served with the US Air Force until the early 1950s.

Formation

Fighters such as the Mustang flew together in small groups. This was called flying in formation. Pilots in formation could keep an eye on each other and defend each other in case they were attacked.

Propeller

P-51 MUSTANG

Length: 9.8 metres

Wingspan: 11.3 metres

Weight: 3.5 tonnes

Engine: Packard V-12

Top speed: 708 kilometres per hour

Ceiling: 12,800 metres

Armament: 6 Browning machine guns /**rockets**

Number built: more than 15,000

First flight: October 1940

Recording kills

Mustang pilots (and pilots of other fighters) would paint symbols on their planes to show how many enemy planes they had shot down. The pilot of this Mustang has claimed eight German kills. Mustang pilots claimed to have shot down nearly 5,000 enemy planes during World War II.

FIRST JET FIGHTERS

Until the 1930s, all fighter planes were powered by propellers turned by engines that had pistons moving up and down in cylinders (which work like the engines on a car). But propeller-driven planes can't fly at very high altitudes, where the air is thin, and they can't fly super-fast. Jet-powered planes can fly both high and fast, so the invention of the jet engine in the 1930s, in Germany and England, was a vital step in the development of fighter planes.

Extra thrust

Afterburners boost the power of a fighter's jet engines. They squirt fuel into the hot gases in the exhaust, creating more hot gases. Afterburners enable quick take-offs and fast climbs.

MESSERSCHMITT ME 262

The German Me 262 was the first jet-powered fighter to go into battle. It first flew in 1942, during World War II, but didn't enter service until 1944 because of problems with its new jet engines. The Me 262 was successful at attacking **Allied** bombers, but it came too late to make a difference.

ME 262

Length: 10.6 metres

Wingspan: 12.6 metres

Weight: 3.8 tonnes

Engines: twin Junkers Jumo 004 turbojets

Top speed: 900 kilometres per hour

Ceiling: 11,450 metres

Armament: 4 x 30 mm cannon plus 24 rockets

Number built: 1,430

First flight: July 1942

Number of kills: 542

JET ENGINE

A jet engine works by sending a fast-moving jet of hot gases from its exhaust nozzle. This pushes the engine, and the plane it's attached to, forward.

Fuel burns in combustion chamber

Hot gases stream out of nozzle

Compressor squeezes air

Turbine turns the compressor

Air intake

Turbojet engine

Hot gases turn the turbine

STEALTHY
MACHINES

Many modern fighters, such as the Lockheed Martin F-22 Raptor and the Lockheed Martin F-35 Lightning, feature 'stealth' technology. This technology makes it more difficult for a fighter to be detected by sensors, such as radar sensors and infra-red (heat) sensors. Ground defences, other aircraft and homing missiles employ these sensors to detect, track and attack fighter aircraft. Being stealthy allows fighters to reach their targets without being spotted and attacked.

Lockheed F-117A Nighthawk

The amazing angular design of the Lockheed F-117A remained top secret for many years. This was the world's first fighter to be equipped with stealth technology, and was nicknamed the 'Stealth Fighter'.

The F-117A made its maiden flight in 1981 and started operating with the US Air Force in 1983. It flew many missions during the Iraq War of 1991, and finally retired from service in 2008. The F-117's peculiar shape made it too tricky for pilots to control by hand, so it was flown by a computer.

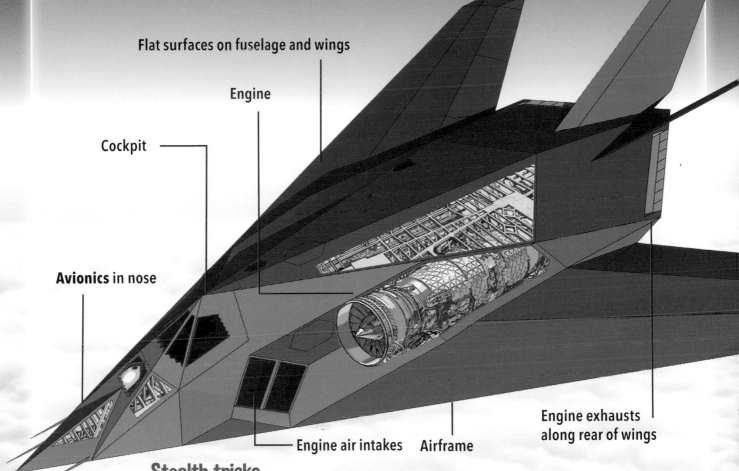

Flat surfaces on fuselage and wings

Engine

Cockpit

Avionics in nose

Engine air intakes   Airframe

Engine exhausts along rear of wings

Stealth tricks

The fuselage and wings of the F-117A were faceted (divided into flat panels) to make it virtually invisible to radar. When radar waves hit the F-117A, they bounced off, but hardly ever back towards the radar detector. The aircraft also had radar-absorbing paint to reduce the number of waves that bounced off. The engine nozzles were designed to hide the hot engine exhaust that could give away the plane's position to heat sensors, such as those on **air-to-air missiles**.

F-117A

Length:	20.1 metres
Wingspan:	13.2 metres
Weight:	13.4 tonnes
Engines:	twin General Electric turbofans
Top speed:	993 kilometres per hour
Ceiling:	13,716 metres
Armament:	1 x 20 mm cannon, missiles
Number built:	64
First flight:	June 1981

AT THE
CONTROLS

Taking the controls of a state-of-the-art fighter plane is a dream for many pilots. Fighter pilots must obviously be great at flying, and often at high speed, hugging the ground. But they must also be able to process massive amounts of information coming from their aircraft's systems, to think fast and make quick decisions if they are to complete their missions and return safely. This all takes years of training.

In the cockpit

The controls of a modern fighter are 'fly-by-wire', or 'fly-by-light'. The pilot steers the plane, but a computer controls the engine and flight surfaces (the rudder, elevators, etc.) using electronic or light signals. Navigation instruments show the terrain below, even when it's cloudy. Weapons systems detect, track and target enemy aircraft and ground target.

Flying suit and helmet

During high-speed turns, pilots experience an effect called high-g. This causes blood to drain from the head to the legs, which can lead to blackouts. To counteract this, pilots wear a g-suit, which squeezes their legs to stop too much blood flowing into them. The flying helmet contains headphones, a microphone and maybe a computer display and sensors that track where the pilot is looking.

Pilot is released from seat to parachute to ground

Parachute opens

Rockets propel seat away from plane

Canopy is blown off, then a catapult fires the seat up and out

Ejector seat

The pilot's seat can be a lifesaver. In an emergency, if the pilot thinks the aircraft is going to crash, he or she pulls a handle on the seat, and the seat is blasted out of the cockpit, with the pilot still strapped in.

Simulator

A flight simulator recreates what it is like to fly an aircraft, but without the danger. The simulator creates the world outside the cockpit using computer graphics, and twists and rolls the cockpit around with hydraulic rams. Fighter pilots learn to fly particular fighters (this simulator is for an F-16 Flying Falcon) using simulators, and also practise how to deal with emergency situations and use new weapons.

TARGETING
WEAPONS

Fighter planes would be useless without their weapons. Most modern fighters are multi-role aircraft, which means they can be fighters, fighter-bombers or ground-attack aircraft. So they can carry an array of different weapons for attacking different targets. These weapons include cannon and anti-aircraft missiles for attacking other aircraft; ground-attack missiles for destroying tanks; and rockets, **laser**-guided bombs and sometimes also anti-ship missiles.

Firing a missile

A missile is a self-propelled weapon that is guided to its target. It has a rocket motor that pushes it along. Different guidance systems use lasers, **radar** and infra-red light to guide missiles. The guidance system can be on the aircraft (called remote guidance) or on the missile itself (called homing guidance). For example, in an infra-red homing missile (also called a heat-seeking missile), the missile detects heat from its target, and keeps adjusting its steering fins so that it is travelling towards the heat source.

Night sights

At night, pilots pick out their targets using a night sight, also known as an image intensifier. This system uses an infra-red camera, which forms a picture using the heat coming from objects on the ground. Hotter objects appear brighter in the image. The images appear on cockpit screens or a display inside the pilot's helmet (see p. 20).

Weapons pylons

Most missiles are carried under a fighter's wings, in places called weapons stations (shown left on a Sukhoi Su-34). At each station there is a connector called a pylon, and each pylon is suitable for a particular weapon. The weapons are locked to the pylons until they are fired. Pylons and weapons can be changed so that the fighter can attack different sorts of targets on different missions.

Sukhoi Su-34

ATTACK
HELICOPTERS

Attack helicopters, also known as helicopter gunships, such as the Boeing Apache and Mil Mi-24, possess deadly firepower. They carry out attacks on targets on the ground. Helicopters have the advantage that they can hover close to their targets, and operate from bases without runways. They carry similar weapons to fighter planes, but also powerful machine guns.

Boeing AH-64D Apache Longbow

This twin-engined attack helicopter's main role is to destroy enemy armaments, such as tanks and mobile guns. The pilot sits in the front cockpit, and the co-pilot (who is also the gunner) sits in the rear cockpit, above and behind the pilot. The Apache carries rockets, and its powerful machine gun can be 'slaved' to the gunner's helmet. This means it is aimed by movements of the gunner's head. Apache pilots fly low, using hills and valleys for cover, a tactic known as terrain masking.

Apache AH-64

Length: 17.7 metres

Rotor diameter: 14.6 metres

Weight: 5.2 tonnes

Engines: Twin General Electric turboshafts

Top speed: 293 kilometres per hour

Ceiling: 6,400 metres

Armament: 1 x machine gun, missiles, rockets

Number built: more than 2,000

First flight: September 1975

Flares for defence

Attack helicopters are vulnerable to attack from missiles fired from aircraft and the ground. If a helicopter is targeted by heat-seeking missiles, the pilots can fire off flares to confuse the missile. These helicopters can also pull off radical moves if needed (below).

F-35
FIGHTER

The Lockheed Martin F-35 Lightning is a 5th generation fighter jet (each major advance in fighter technology brings in a new generation of fighter jet). It is one of the most modern fighters, featuring stealth technology, fly-by-wire controls, advanced digital avionics (aviation electronics), an array of sensors, and high-speed communications. It is very agile, but can also fly at supersonic speeds.

Engine

Lift fan door

Ejection seat

Lift fan

Drive shaft from engine

Radar

Engine nozzle

During forward flight, the rear engine exhaust points backwards. The lift fan duct is closed to give the fuselage a smooth shape.

Elevon (elevator and aileron combined)

Engine nozzle tilts down for STOVL

Roll nozzle

Multiple roles

The F-35 has been designed to perform many different jobs. There are three main models, or variants:

F-35A

This is a high-performance multi-role fighter. It is a CTOL (conventional take-off and landing) aircraft, which operates from airbases with runways.

F-35B

The F-35B is an STOVL (short take-off and vertical landing) aircraft. It needs only a short runway for take-off, and can land vertically. It operates from small bases and from the decks of aircraft carriers.

F-35C

This variant is designed for taking off and landing on the restricted flight decks of aircraft carriers, and it has strengthened undercarriage for hard landings. It is a long-range strike fighter, for attacking ground targets.

STOVL operations

For short take-offs and for vertical landings, the F-35B has a lift fan behind the cockpit. A door above the fan opens, and the fan is connected to the engine. The fan forces air downwards, pushing the plane upwards. At the same time, the engine exhaust tilts downwards, adding to the upwards push. After take-off, the engine exhaust points backwards, the fan switches off and the F-35B starts to fly forwards, using its wings for lift.

TIMELINE

1936
The Supermarine Spitfire makes its maiden flight

1942
The Messerschmitt Me 262 becomes the first jet fighter

1903
The Wright Brothers perform the first controlled, powered flight with their plane Flyer

1939
World War II begins

1945
World War II ends

1961
The last Spitfire retires from duty

1917
The Fokker Dr.1, a German triplane, makes it first flight

1918
The fighter ace Baron Manfred von Richthofen is killed in combat

1937
The first jet engine is developed

1942
The P-51 Mustang takes off for the first time

1915
The first flight of the Airco DH.2 pusher plane

1935
The Messerschmitt Bf 109 makes its maiden flight

1940
British and German fighters engage each other in the Battle of Britain

1914
World War I begins; countries start to build fighter planes

1974
The General Dynamics F-16 becomes the first fighter to take off with fly-by-wire controls

1986
The Apache AH-64 attack helicopter enters service with the US Army

2006
The Lockheed Martin F-35 makes its first test flight

1981
The F-117A Nighthawk stealth fighter makes its first flight

FACT FILE

One of World War II's best fighters, the De Havilland Mosquito, was made entirely from wood.

The gunner of the Apache AH-64 has a special helmet linked to the helicopter's gun. The gun aims where the gunner looks.

During World War I, Manfred von Richthofen led a group of German pilots known as the Flying Circus. Von Richthofen alone shot down 80 aircraft before he was killed in 1918.

In 1944, Germany built a rocket-powered fighter: the Messerschmitt 163 Komet. This tiny plane could fly at more than 1,000 kilometres per hour.

The life expectancy of a Spitfire pilot who fought in the Battle of Britain was just four weeks.

The engine of an F-35 produces enough push to lift a 20-tonne weight.

The Lockheed F-117A first flew in 1981, but its existence was kept top secret until 1988.

The Mustang carried enough fuel to allow it to fly from Britain to Germany and back, protecting bombers on bombing raids.

GLOSSARY

Ace
A fighter pilot who shoots down many enemy planes

Aileron
A control surface (like a hinged flap) on the tailplane of an aircraft, used to tilt the aircraft's nose up or down

Air superiority
Having control of the air over a battlefield, so that enemy planes can't fly

Air-to-air missile
A missile fired from a plane in the air to attack a target also in the air

Air-to-surface missile
A missile fired from a plane in the air to attack a target on the ground

Allies
The combined forces of Britain, the United States and other countries during World War I and World War II

Altitude
The distance that a plane is above sea level

Avionics
Short for aviation electronics, which are all the electronics needed for flying and navigating a modern plane

Biplane
A plane with two pairs of wings, one above the other

Ceiling
The maximum height at which a particular plane can fly

Drag
The resistance that the air makes on a plane as the plane flies through the air

Elevator
A control surface (like a hinged flap) on the wings of an aircraft, used to roll the aircraft from side to side

Fuselage
The main body of an aicraft

Eddie Rickenbacker, World War I ace (see p.11)

In-line engine
An engine in which the cylinders are arranged in a line

Laser
An intense beam of light

Monoplane
A plane with just one pairs of wings (most modern planes are monoplanes)

Radar
A device that detects objects by emitting radio waves and sensing them bounce back

Radial engine
An engine in which the cylinders are arranged in a circle

Range
The maximum distance that an aircraft can fly before getting short of fuel

Rocket
An unguided missile

Rotary engine
An engine in which the cylinders are arranged in a circle and rotate with the propeller

Rudder
A control surface (like a hinged flap) on the fin of an aircraft, used to make the aircraft turn from side to side

Stealthy
An aircraft with stealth technology, which makes it hard for enemy forces to detect

Strut
A rigid rod that keeps parts of a structure in place

Triplane
A plane with three pairs of wings, one above the other

Wingspan
The distance from one wing tip to the other on a plane

An air-to-air missile suspended under the wing of a Russian fighter plane

INDEX

A
afterburners 16
Airco DH.2 8
Apache helicopter 24–25

B
balloons 9
Battle of Britain 12–13
Boeing AH-64D Apache Longbow 24–25

C
cockpits 13, 20

D
dogfights 11

E
ejector seat 21

F
fighter pilots 6, 7, 8, 10–11, 15, 20–21, 23, 25, 26
Fokker Dr.1 10

G
g-suit 20

H
helicopters 24–25
helmets 20, 23
high-g 20

I
interrupter gear 10

J
jet engine 17
jet fighters, first 16–17

L
Lockheed F-117A Nighthawk 18–19
Lockheed Martin F-22 Raptor 6
Lockheed Martin F-35 Lightning 18, 26–27

M
Messerschmitt Bf 109 13
Messerschmitt ME 262 17
missiles 22, 25

N
night sights 23

P
P–51 Mustang 14–15
propellers 8, 10, 16
pusher planes 8

R
rotary engine 9

S
simulators 21
Sopwith Triplane 6, 7
Spitfire 12–13
stealth fighters 18–19
STOVL operations 27
Sukhoi Su-34 23

T
types of fighter plane 6

W
weapon pylons 23
weapons 22–23
World War I 6, 8, 9, 10–11
World War II 12–13, 14, 15, 17
Wright Flyer 9

The Author

Chris Oxlade is an experienced author of educational books for children, with more than 200 titles to his name, including many on science and technology. He enjoys camping and adventurous outdoor sports, including rock climbing, hill running, kayaking and sailing. He lives in England with his wife, children and dogs.

Picture Credits (abbreviations: t = top; b = bottom; c = centre; l = left; r = right)
© www.shutterstock.com: 1bc, 2bl, 4c, 12c, 20l, 29tr, 30-31bc, 31tr.
3, c = KEYSTONE Pictures USA / Alamy Stock Photo. 6-7, c = US Air Force Photo / Alamy Stock Photo. 7, t = Andrew Harker / Alamy Stock Photo. 8, c = Angus McComiskey / Alamy Stock Photo. 9, t = Peter Wheeler / Alamy Stock Photo. 9, c = Ian Dagnall / Alamy Stock Photo. 9, b = World History Archive / Alamy Stock Photo. 10, b = Real Window Gallery / Alamy Stock Photo. 10-11, c = Antony Nettle / Alamy Stock Photo. 11, b = The Granger Collection / Alamy Stock Photo. 13, t = Trinity Mirror / Mirrorpix / Alamy Stock Photo. 13, b = Antony Nettle / Alamy Stock Photo. 15, t = Antony Nettle / Alamy Stock Photo. 15, b = CBW / Alamy Stock Photo. 16, b = Stocktrek Images, Inc. / Alamy Stock Photo. 16-17, c = age fotostock / Alamy Stock Photo. 18-19, c = age fotostock / Alamy Stock Photo. 21, cl = A. T. Willet / Alamy Stock Photo. 21, b = US Airforce Photo / Alamy Stock Photo. 22-23, c = Stocktrek Images, Inc. / Alamy Stock Photo. 23, t = PhotoEdit / Alamy Stock Photo. 23, b = Stocktrek Images, Inc. /Alamy Stock Photo. 24-25, c = robert Leyland / Alamy Stock Photo. 26, b = Mint Photography / Alamy Stock Photo. 27, b = Lockheed Martin. 29, b = Granger Historical Picture Archive / Alamy Stock Photo.